Adaptation

Steve Parker

Heinemann
LIBRARY

www.heinemann.co.uk
Visit our website to find out more information about Heinemann Library books.

To order:

 Phone 44 (0) 1865 888066

Send a fax to 44 (0) 1865 314091

 Visit the Heinemann Bookshop at www.heinemann.co.uk to browse our catalogue and order online.

First published in Great Britain by Heinemann Library,
Halley Court, Jordan Hill, Oxford OX2 8EJ
a division of Reed Educational and Professional Publishing Ltd.
Heinemann is a registered trademark of Reed Educational & Professional Publishing Ltd.

OXFORD MELBOURNE AUCKLAND
JOHANNESBURG BLANTYRE GABORONE
IBADAN PORTSMOUTH (NH) USA CHICAGO

Designed by Celia Floyd
Originated by Dot Gradations
Printed by Wing King Tong, in Hong Kong

ISBN 0 431 10884 6
04 03 02 01 00
10 9 8 7 6 5 4 3 2 1

British Library Cataloguing in Publication Data

Parker, Steve 1952-
    Adaptation. - (Life processes)
    1. Adaptation (Ecology) - Juvenile literature
    I. Title
    578.4

Acknowledgements

The Publishers would like to thank the following for permission to reproduce photographs:

Bruce Coleman Collection: Mary Plage pg.14; *Corbis*: Daniel Samuel Robbins pg.9; *NHPA*: pg.20, NA Callow pg.4, David Middleton pg.4, A.N.T. pg.7, pg.24, Darek Karp pg.8, Stephen Dalton pg.10, pg.16, pg.28, Anthony Bannister pg.11, pg.25, Martin Harvey pg.12, pg.15, Dr Eckart Pott pg.13, Hellio & Van Ingen pg.17, GJ Cambridge pg.18, EA Janes pg.19, Roy Waller pg.19, Norbert Wu pg.21, B & C Alexander pg.22, John Shaw pg.23, Daniel Heuclin pg.25, David Hosking pg.27, Vincente Gardia Canseco pg.29; *Oxford Scientific Films*: Daniel J Cox pg.4, Colin Milkins pg.6, Michael Fogden pg.10, Richard Herrmann pg.20, Roland Mayr pg.26, Sean Morris pg.27.

Cover photograph reproduced with permission of Tony Stone.

Every effort has been made to contact copyright holders of any material reproduced in this book. Any omissions will be rectified in subsequent printings if notice is given to the Publisher.

Any words appearing in the text in bold, **like this**, are explained in the glossary.

Contents

Introduction

The living world is packed with incredible variety and diversity. Living things, called **organisms**, vary from jelly-like microbes to worms and insects, flowers and fish, lizards and birds, massive whales and giant trees. But most organisms cannot live just anywhere. Each living thing has features that allow it to survive in certain types of surroundings, called its **habitat**. These features are known as **adaptations**. Each living thing is suited, or adapted, to its habitat.

A variety of habitats

The world has many different types of **habitats**, such as mountains, lakes, woods and seashores. Most animals, plants and other living things are **adapted** to one particular habitat. This is so common and natural that we rarely notice it. But if we picture a living thing in the wrong habitat, the idea of adaptation becomes more obvious.

The dolphin's smooth, streamlined body slips at speed through the sea.

Suppose that a dolphin and a camel suddenly swapped places. The dolphin would not last long in a baking desert, with no water and too much heat. A camel could not survive in the open sea. It can hardly swim and would soon drown. Neither type of animal is adapted to the other's habitat.

Small creatures like shieldbugs are coloured to blend into their surroundings so that they are noticed less by **predators**.

Needs for survival

Living things have certain needs or requirements from their habitat, if they are to survive. These include:

- Energy to power their bodily life processes. Plants obtain their energy from sunlight and animals get theirs from food.
- Raw materials and **nutrients** for growth, body maintenance and repair. Animals get these from food and plants from air and soil.
- Oxygen, the invisible gas in the air around us. Almost all living things need oxygen to survive.
- Water – life cannot exist without it.
- Shelter and protection from bad conditions such as harsh weather, and also from predators.
- A mate for breeding. This is not vital for an individual to stay alive, but it is essential if its kind, or **species**, is to continue.

Coniferous tree branches can flex and slope down so that snow slips off, without piling up and breaking the tree.

In each habitat living things face problems in obtaining these needs. This book shows how they have adapted to solve the problems and survive in the many different habitats on Earth.

On the move

One example of an adaptation is a body feature that enables an animal to move effectively in its habitat. For example:
- A fish has a broad tail and fins to push itself through the water.
- A bird has flapping wings to carry it through the air.
- A mole has broad, strong front paws to dig through soil.
- A gazelle has long legs to run at speed across the grasslands.
- A monkey has long, flexible limbs with grasping hands and feet, to swing through the forest branches.

Changing conditions

Conditions in a **habitat** are always changing. Each day the Sun rises bringing light and warmth. The weather brings changes such as winds, storms, frost and snow. On the seashore the tides rise and fall. These are all changes in the non-living world. Changes also happen in the living world. Sometimes animals like locusts, lemmings or rabbits breed in vast numbers. They eat so much that other animals, who normally eat the same food, begin to starve. If living things are to survive, they must cope with all these varying conditions.

The barnacle's life is ruled by the twice-daily rise and fall of the tides.

Hot and cold

One of the main changes every day is the rise and fall in temperature, which happens as the Sun rises and sets. Most animals are **cold-blooded** and their activity is greatly affected by the surrounding temperature. After a cool night, a snake crawls slowly into the morning Sun and basks in its rays. Soon the snake is warm enough to move fast and pursue prey. As dusk falls and the temperature drops, the snake cools down again and can only move slowly. So it hides under a sheltering rock for the night.

Similar animals, different adaptations

There are many examples of similar creatures, from the same animal group, that are **adapted** to different habitats.

● The African hare and American jackrabbit have very long legs and ears, and short fur. These features help the hare's body to lose warmth in the very hot conditions of its desert home.

● The Arctic hare has shorter legs and ears, and very long, thick fur. These features help to prevent loss of body warmth in the very cold habitat of the far north.

Adapted to the dark

Each day also brings changes in light levels, which affect many living things. Some animals are **nocturnal**, that is, active at night. They include moths, mice, owls and bats. They are adapted to finding their way in the dark by various means, such as the owl's extra-large eyes or the bat's high-pitched squeaking sounds that bounce off nearby objects.

Mice have huge eyes and long whiskers as adaptations to being nocturnal.

Types of adaptations

- Overall shape – A worm is long and thin to burrow through soil. A leaf is broad and flat to catch most sunlight.
- Colour and pattern – The green tree frog is coloured to sit unnoticed among green leaves.
- Body parts – A part of the body may be adapted for a certain task, like the long fangs of a viper which stab venom (poison) into its prey.
- Internal workings – The chemical life processes of a living thing may show adaptations. The presence of a natural chemical **anti-freeze** in the bodies of ice-worms allows them to live in the freezing temperatures inside glaciers.

Similar adaptations, different animals

There are many examples of varied creatures, from different animal groups, which have similar adaptations because they live in the same habitat.

- Frogs, lizards and squirrels that live in trees have long, slim, grasping fingers to hold on to the branches.
- Frogs, lizards and squirrels that live on the ground have shorter, stubbier fingers to walk and run on hard surfaces.

Life in the mountains

Compared to the surrounding lowlands, mountains are generally cold, wet and windy. Very tall mountains have snow and ice on the upper slopes. Also the air becomes thinner or less dense with height, so there is less of the vital gas oxygen that living things need to breathe. So the higher a mountain, the more severe the conditions for life. Mountain animals and plants are **adapted** in many ways to withstand these tough conditions.

Lower plant zones

On many mountains, plants grow at certain levels or zones. There are broadleaved woodlands at the base. The foothills are cloaked with conifer trees that have thin, tough, needle-like leaves to survive long, cold winters. Increasing cold, snow and wind mean that tall trees cannot survive above a certain height, called the tree line. So the next highest zone may be bushy scrub with hardy plants such as heathers. These have tough leaves and woody stems that are less damaged by the strong winds.

Did you know?
- Yaks have the longest fur of any mammal, growing up to a metre in length.
- Plants such as edelweiss have fine hairs on their leaves to keep out cold and keep in moisture.

The alpine pasque flower, like the edelweiss, is adapted to harsh mountain conditions.

Up and down

Many larger mountain animals, like chamois in Europe and yak in Asia, make yearly journeys called **migrations**. They walk up to the higher slopes in spring where the alpine meadow plants grow quickly in the summer warmth. In autumn they return to the lower slopes and the shelter of the forests. **Predators** such as wolves and snow leopards follow them on the journey.

Yaks are adapted to living high up in the Himalaya mountains.

Higher plant zones

Above the scrub zone are short grasses and herbs – the alpine meadow. These are low-growing with cushion or rosette shapes, to avoid the fierce winds. Many alpine plants like edelweiss and giant groundsel have developed adaptations like hairy leaves to keep out the worst of the frost and also to keep in moisture, since the soil is thin and rain soon races away down the steep slopes. Higher still among the icy rocks and crags, no types of plant can survive.

Mountain animals

Small creatures such as insects and spiders can survive in the high mountains by feeding on bits and pieces of dead plants and animals, blown up the slopes by strong winds. Birds such as condors soar over the peaks watching for dead or dying victims. Mountain mammals such as chinchillas and vicunas in South America, and yak in Asia, have very long, thick fur to keep in body warmth. Like the mountain goat, chamois and Siberian ibex, they have strong legs and feet to grip the slippery rocks and ice as they move at speed across the steep slopes.

In the forest

Regions with a moist tropical climate have ideal conditions for plant life. There is year-round warmth and light, plenty of water, and minerals and **nutrients** in the soil. The thriving variety of plants in turn supports a vast range of animals, making tropical forests the richest **habitats** on Earth for wildlife. However, there are other kinds of forests where conditions are less favourable. Living things here have very different **adaptations**.

The macaw's bright colours and loud squawking warn other birds that this patch of tropical forest is occupied.

Plentiful life

The tropical rainforest habitat is perfect for life in all shapes, forms and colours. Plants and animals do not have to battle for survival against the physical conditions. But so many life-forms packed so close together means an abundance of **predators**, **parasites**, competitors for food, shelter and living space, and rivals for breeding. So living things must battle with each other rather than with the physical conditions.

The ground in a tropical forest is dark, so **epiphytic** plants like these bromeliads grow high up among the branches nearer the light.

Coping with cold

In **temperate** regions, winter is shutdown time. Broad-leaved trees lose their leaves. Small animals like insects die off and leave tough-cased eggs to survive the cold. Dormice, marmots and similar creatures **hibernate** or go into a deep winter sleep. Squirrels rest in their nests, coming out occasionally to dig up nuts and other food that they buried in autumn. Some small birds such as swifts and warblers **migrate**, flying long distances to warmer regions. All of these are adaptations to survive the cold of winter.

Frozen solid

In the far north and south, winters are even longer and colder. Conifer trees like pines, firs and spruces are adapted to these severe climates. Their leaves are small, tough and resist frost and icy winds. Their sloping branches allow snow to slip off before it becomes too heavy and breaks the tree.

Animals also have many ways of surviving these long winters. Frogs such as the spring peeper, striped chorus and grey tree frogs, also the Siberian salamander, and reptiles like painted turtles, can all withstand being frozen almost solid. Their bodies have high levels of **anti-freeze** substances so they can thaw back to life in the spring.

How to hide in the forest

Many animals show amazing adaptations for **camouflage** by resembling parts of trees and bushes. They blend into the forest surroundings and are less obvious to predators or prey.

- Stick insects look like twigs.
- Leaf insects resemble green forest leaves.
- Thornbugs and scalebugs are shaped like tree thorns.
- Moths or butterflies resting on tree trunks look like bark or old leaves.
- Spiders and mantises have bright colours to blend in with flowers.

Looper caterpillars 'freeze' still to look like bugs or small twigs. A spider has not recognized this caterpillar.

Rolling grasslands

Where the climate is too dry for trees, but too moist for a desert, grasses grow. They cover the land as far as the eye can see. The grassland **habitat** supports a huge quantity of life. However, animals have few trees or bushes to provide shade and shelter, and many struggle to survive the long, dry season. There is also the ever-present risk of a bushfire or a sudden flood when the rains come.

Large plains mammals like pronghorn in North America, and giraffes and eland (the largest antelope) in Africa, have long legs to race away from predators.

The prairies

On the grasslands or **prairies** of North America, the largest animals are bison. Being grazers they have wide, flat teeth for munching grass all day. Their huge size, and living together in herds, are **adaptations** for self-defence against **predators** such as wolves. Like many large grazers, bison **migrate** from a dry region to find better grazing elsewhere. At least, they once did. Bison numbers were hugely reduced by human hunters and the prairies are now used for farming. On African grasslands, called savannah, zebra and wildebeest have similar herd-dwelling lives.

Big birds

Grasslands and open scrub are home to the world's largest birds. These are ostriches in Africa, emus in Australia and rheas on the pampas (grasslands) of South America. None of these birds can fly. But all have long, powerful legs to run at speed and escape from predators, and sharp toe claws to kick out in defence.

Living low down

Smaller grassland animals have less defence against predators. So many dig tunnels and burrows. In North America prairie dogs form huge underground townships. As they feed on the surface a few prairie dogs are always watching for danger. They yip and bark if a hawk, fox or similar predator comes near.

Dung beetles collect and bury dung from grassland mammals as food for their developing grubs.

African naked mole rats stay in their tunnel networks all of their lives. These strange mammals live in a **colony** like bees or ants. Only one female, the 'queen', breeds. The others are 'workers' who dig tunnels and gather plant roots and other food.

City in the countryside

Termites are small, pale, thin-skinned insects that would soon die in hot sun. So they adapt small patches of grassland for their own needs. They build a tall mound from mud that dries hard, and dig a huge nest underneath. Here a million or more termites live in a cool, moist, underground city. Snakes, foxes and even cheetahs use the mounds for shelter, and owls and other birds perch on them.

Did you know?

Some animals and plants, such as acacia trees and ants have special relationships. The ants bite and sting animals who try to eat the tree's leaves. In return, the thorny acacia provides the ants with a protected place to live. This type of relationship, where both partners benefit, is called **symbiosis**.

Flowing waters

A typical river is not one **habitat** but many. In the hills, its gathering waters rush fast and foaming over a stony bed. When the river reaches lower plains it flows in wide loops, or **meanders**, and its current decreases so that sand and silt collect along its banks. As it enters the sea at its mouth or **estuary**, it slows still further and its fresh-water mixes with salty seawater. Different animals and plants are **adapted** to these different parts of the river.

The young river

Near the river's start the fast current sweeps away small plants, animals and bits of food. However, a few animals are suited to these conditions. Stonefly **larvae** (young) have low, flattened bodies and strong, wide-set, clawed legs to grip the pebbles on the bottom. Fish called bullheads also have low, flat bodies and hide among the stones too, where the river flow is slower.

Dippers are land birds, but have adapted to diving for food in fast-flowing upland streams.

The mature river

As the river's waters slow, **nutrient**-rich mud collects on the bottom and bank. Plants such as reeds and rushes take root, providing food and shelter. Larger predatory fish like perch and pike thrive here, eating the plentiful smaller prey of worms, water insects and young fish. Catfish and crayfish come out from their holes at night to **scavenge**.

The estuary

Near the sea, the fresh river water mixes with the sea's salty water. Salty water can cause great problems for freshwater animals since it greatly affects their body chemistry. Certain, fish such as mullet, are adapted to this in-between watery world. So are shellfish like winkles, oysters and mussels.

Mangrove swamps

Along some sheltered tropical coasts, mangroves form huge swamps. The thick seashore mud contains little oxygen. But mangrove trees have roots that stick up into the air and water, to take in extra oxygen. Mudskippers are also adapted to this habitat. These small fish hold pools of water in their large **gill** chambers, so they can survive in air for many minutes. Their front fins are like muscular 'arms' and they use them to skitter across the mudflats.

Many big fish such as sharks and rays swim into coastal mangrove swamps, to lay their eggs in the sheltered waters.

Did you know?

The world's largest reptile lives in coastal areas such as estuaries and mangrove swamps, mainly around the Indian and west Pacific Oceans. This is the saltwater or estuarine crocodile, which grows more than eight metres long.

Lakes and ponds

Compared to a fast river, the still water of a lake or pool does not have the problems of a fast current and few places to shelter. But cold, moving water takes in or dissolves more oxygen from the air than the warm, still water. Tropical lakes and marshes may look ideal for wildlife, but animals and plants find survival difficult in the **stagnant**, oxygen-poor water.

Rat-tailed maggots (**larvae** of hoverflies) survive in stagnant water by breathing air through a long tail tube.

Breathing

Creatures get around the breathing problem with various **adaptations**. In the Amazon's tropical swamps some fish can gulp air into their **swim bladders** or guts. The blood-rich linings of these body parts absorb oxygen from the swallowed air, like the lungs of a land animal. One of the world's biggest freshwater fish, the arapaima (pirarucu) which grows more than two metres long, uses this method.

Lungfish have body parts that are even more adapted for breathing air, almost like real lungs. They live in South America, Africa and Australia. They are long, slim fish resembling eels. They grow to about 1.5 metres long and hunt smaller fish, frogs and other water creatures. They absorb oxygen from air when their pools become shallow and stagnant.

Water in swamps and creeks is often muddy and cloudy, so hunting by sight is difficult. In Australia the platypus grubs in the mud for small animals using its sensitive duck-like beak. This detects tiny electrical currents given off naturally by the active muscles of its prey.

Did you know?

In South America the electric eel can give a shock of 500-plus volts from its muscles, to stun its victim. This fish is not a real eel but a member of the carp group.

Blood red

On a much smaller scale, worms called blood- or sludge-worms (tubifex) also survive in low-oxygen water, even polluted ponds. They live half-buried in tubes on the bottom, their bright tail ends waving in the water. The red colour is caused by extra amounts in their blood of the oxygen-carrying substance **haemoglobin**. (This is the same substance that makes our blood red.)

Adapted for lurking

Air-breathing animals of lakes and swamps do not face the problem of low oxygen levels in water. But they still need to obtain food. The top **predators** are crocodiles and alligators. Their body shape is adapted to lurking almost submerged in water. The nostrils and eyes on the top of the head allow the crocodile to breathe, smell and watch for prey. Its long jaws and many teeth grab victims in a vice-like grip. These supreme hunters have been around for more than 200 million years, since the time of the dinosaurs.

The flamingo's special beak has comb-like flaps inside to strain food from water and mud.

17

Tides and waves

Coasts and seashores have the world's most varying conditions. Twice each day the sea level rises at high tide and floods the area with salty water. Waves crash onto the shore with massive force. As the tide falls, living things are exposed to hot Sun, drying winds, the fresh-water of rain, or icy frosts. Added to all this are the usual changes of day and night and the yearly cycle of seasons. Seashore plants and animals have extremely specialized **adaptations** and most cannot live anywhere else.

Shore-fish like blennies and shannies have tough, rubbery, slippery skin to avoid being damaged by waves and rolling boulders.

Tough plants

Plants along the coast are mainly types of **algae** called seaweeds. They do not have proper roots like land plants but many have root-like holdfasts that cling strongly to the rocks so they are not swept away by waves. They also have leaf-like fronds with tough, leathery, slippery surfaces that are not torn by the waves or dried out by the Sun.

Ruled by the tide

Most seashore animals are not adapted to the 24-hour cycle of day and night, like animals on land. They follow the 12-hour rise and fall of the tides. Crabs, shrimps, prawns, sea-snails like winkles and whelks, and worms such as ragworms are all active at high tide and hide away for low tide.

Some animals stay under the mud or sand. They include shellfish like tellins, cockles, clams and gapers. As the tide comes in they extend fleshy tubes called **siphons**. They suck in water through one siphon, filter out tiny edible particles inside their bodies and squirt the water out of the other siphon.

Sea-anemones extend their tentacles to catch prey, then as the tide falls they close up like blobs of jelly.

Holding onto the rocks

Like seashore plants, the animals are at risk of being swept away. Crabs, fish and other active animals find shelter in crevices or among seaweeds. Sea-snails have a broad 'foot' for sticking to the rocks. The limpet has the strongest grip and does not need to find shelter. It can clamp its low, cone-shaped shell to the rock with a force that resists the strongest waves.

At low tide seaweeds such as wracks provide cool, moist shelter for seashore animals like this crab.

Trapped for life

On the shore the tides, waves and currents continually bring seawater containing two of life's essentials – food and oxygen. Piddocks are shellfish that burrow into solid rock by twisting and rasping their strong, spiny shells. As in other shellfish, two tubes called siphons take in water for feeding and breathing and then squirt it out. The piddock grows as it bores slowly into the rock so that it becomes too big to leave its tunnel.

Did you know?

The lugworm, in its U-shaped burrow, eats sand to digest any **nutrient** particles. It ejects the grains onto the surface above its rear end as squiggly worm casts. In one year a lugworm can eat enough sand to fill a family car!

19

Life in the ocean

The ocean is the largest **habitat** on Earth, bigger than all other habitats added together. Where its warm, shallow waters lap calmly towards a tropical beach, this may seem ideal for life. But the ocean also has huge waves and strong currents. About 500–1000 metres below the surface it is cold and dark so plants, on which animal life depends, cannot grow. This presents many challenges to living things.

Sealions in the warm, tropical waters off the coast of California.

Small plants, big fish

The main plants in the ocean are microscopic **phytoplankton**. They are food for similarly small animals, **zooplankton**. Larger animals have **adaptations** to feed on such tiny food. The biggest fish in the world, the whale shark and basking shark, filter them from the water using frilly, comb-like parts called **rakers**. These are on the **gills**, the breathing parts on the side of a fish's head.

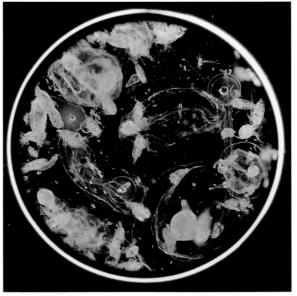

Zooplankton provide a source of food for the whale shark.

Life at the surface

In these huge fish the organ called the liver is enormous and made of very oily flesh. Oil is lighter than water and the large liver helps the fish stay near the surface where plankton is richest. The sperm whale has the opposite problem. It is a mammal and so must surface to breathe air. But its prey of large fish and giant squid live far below in the depths. So the sperm whale has great quantities of a waxy substance, **spermaceti**, in its bulging forehead. As the whale dives this becomes more solid and denser or heavier, helping the whale to descend more than 3000 metres.

On the deep ocean bed

More than seven-eighths of the ocean is not warm and sunlit, but cold and pitch dark. The only food is dead bodies, droppings and other bits drifting down from above. Creatures on the bottom, such as sea-cucumbers, worms, clams and other shellfish are mainly blind. They have no eyes since there is no light to see. Instead, their bodies are very sensitive to touch and water currents. They feed on small edible pieces in the thick seabed mud.

Grab any prey you can

Animals are rare in the vast, black depths of the sea. So deep-sea fish who hunt there are adapted to grab almost any prey they find. The gulper eel has a huge mouth five times bigger than its body. The viperfish has long, sharp teeth that angle backwards into its throat so that any prey it grabs cannot escape.

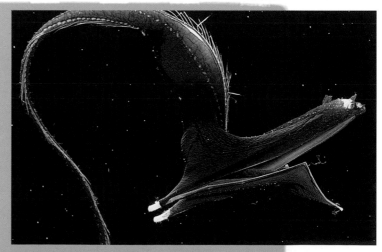

The deep-sea gulper eel showing its huge mouth.

21

Surviv l n ar th pol s

Some of the harshest conditions for life on Earth are found in polar lands. In the far north the ice-covered Arctic Ocean is surrounded by frozen lands and in the south chilly seas surround the ice-covered continent of Antarctica. The main problems are intense cold and long, dark winters. Few plants can grow in such conditions, which means there is little food for animals. The cold, treeless plains of grasses, sedges and other low plants are known as the **tundra habitat**.

Reindeer walk long distances **migrating**, north for summer plant growth, then south for winter shelter.

Short summers, long winters

The polar regions have the most extreme climate in the world. For a short time each summer the Sun never sets and the temperature rises to several degrees above freezing. Conditions are suitable for life. But during the long winter the Sun hardly rises and the air temperature can fall below minus 50° Celsius. Within seconds any living thing would freeze solid.

Summer visitors
The winter in polar lands is too long, cold and dark for most larger animals. So they leave or migrate. In the Arctic many kinds of ducks, geese, plovers and similar birds fly south to warmer regions for the winter. They return north again next spring to nest and raise their young.

Coping with winter

Plants and animals in polar regions have made **adaptations** to cope with the intense winter cold and take advantage of the brief summer growing season. The main plants are sedges and mosses. They are low-growing, out of the fierce wind. Small animals like springtails, midges, mosquitoes and other insects spend the winter as tough-cased eggs that hatch in spring.

Warm white coats

Warm-blooded Arctic animals include birds such as snowy owls and ptarmigan, and mammals like polar bears, seals, voles, lemmings, snowshoe hares and Arctic foxes. They have extra-thick coats of feathers or fur and also a thick layer of fat under the skin, called **blubber**, to keep in body warmth. Most spend the long winter resting in sheltered nests in burrows, caves or dens.

Ptarmigan change their white winter plumage to brown for **camouflage** in summer.

In polar seas

The seas around Antarctica are very cold but also extremely rich in **nutrients** brought up from deeper waters by ocean currents. In summer they support a wide variety of life that starts with the tiny plant and animal varieties of plankton. These are eaten by small fish and shrimp-like creatures known as **krill**. In turn these are eaten by squid, larger fish, penguins, seals and the largest animals on the planet, the great whales.

Did you know?

The largest animals that live permanently on the mainland of Antarctica are tiny springtails (types of insects) that are just a few millimetres long.

Heat and drought

Deserts may be hot or cold, sandy or rocky, windy or calm, in highlands or lowlands. But all deserts have one feature in common — lack of water, or **drought**. Since water is vital for any form of life, deserts pose huge problems for animals and plants. Yet even in these almost waterless wastes, living things have developed amazing **adaptations** and found ways to survive.

The desert comes alive

The desert may look brown and lifeless for years. Then within a few days of rain, plants begin to spring up. They have been inactive or **dormant**, as seeds or as underground plant parts such as bulbs and **corms**. They are called **ephemerals** and are adapted to grow quickly while the soil is moist, producing flowers and seeds.

There are also ephemeral animals. Fairy shrimps survive drought as tough-cased eggs. These hatch quickly, grow into adults in the temporary puddles, and breed to produce the next batch of eggs. Their whole life cycle is over within a few days as the desert dries out once more.

The water-holding frog of Australia survives drought underground in a watery, bag-like cocoon.

Gathering moisture

The overriding problem in the desert is to find water. Plants like cacti spread their long, thin roots far and wide to soak up moisture from a large surface area. Cacti's 'leaves' have become sharp spines — an adaptation to protect against plant-eating animals and moisture loss. Their stems are wide and barrel-shaped to store water. Trees such as acacias and baobabs send roots many metres down into the soil to find moisture far below.

The darkling beetle 'headstands' so its body catches morning dew and mist, which run down into its mouth.

Out at night

Many desert creatures avoid the scorching daytime Sun by coming out during twilight or at night. By day smaller animals like desert mice and kangaroo rats hide in cool burrows. Larger animals such as kangaroos and Arabian oryx rest in the shade of a tree, rock or dune. These creatures obtain most of the moisture they need from their food such as leaves and seeds.

Moving over soft sand

Soft desert sand tends to shift and slip as animals move over it – so various desert creatures have adapted their bodies to different ways of moving.

- Kangaroo rats, gerbils and jerboas have large back feet and leap rather than run.
- The camel has wide feet that spread its body weight and prevent it sinking.
- Desert snakes like the sidewinder move in a sideways fashion almost like waves rippling on the beach. The long body pushes against the sand, giving a larger surface area so the sand grains slip less.

- Desert skinks and sandfish (types of lizards) do not walk on the surface. They wriggle through the sand itself, almost like fish swimming through water.

Dromedary camels in the Sahara Desert.

Living on the edge

A few places in the world seem so harsh and inhospitable that life could not survive. They include the ice and snow of glaciers and icebergs, hot springs where the water almost boils, and deep dark caves. Yet even here, living things have **adapted** and found a way to survive – and in some cases, to thrive. **Organisms** that adapt to these severe conditions have few **predators**, competitors or rivals. This is why extreme **habitats** have few kinds or **species** of inhabitants, but those who can survive do so in great numbers.

Life after death

After a bush fire, **pioneer** plants grow rapidly in the blackened earth. They are not adapted for a long stay. Gradually they are crowded out by slower, steadier growers. However, by this time they have already grown, flowered and scattered their seeds widely.

Large trees such as black spruce, wild ginger and labrador tree have adaptations such as thick bark which resists fire damage. Underground parts of herbs like sage, thyme and rosemary also survive the scorching.

Pioneer plants have sprung up here following a bush fire in Yellowstone National Park, Wyoming.

Did you know?

A new island called Surtsey appeared in the North Atlantic near Iceland in 1963. At first it was bare, hot rock. By the year 2000 more than 1,000 species of plants and animals lived there.

Invading new land

Brand new land, like an ocean island made by a just-erupted underwater volcano, rarely stays empty. Plant seeds blow in the wind, like the *Brachycereus* cactus that grows on new volcanic rocks. Sea creatures such as seals and turtles climb out and leave their **nutrient**-rich droppings. Visiting birds bring tiny eggs and small animals on their bodies, and plant seeds and more nutrients in their droppings. Tiny creatures like mites and spiders also blow on the wind. Gradually the bare land develops into a thriving habitat.

When warmth kills

Grylloblattids are strange insects found in remote mountains such as the North American Rockies. They look like a combination of cockroach and cricket but they are a separate insect group. Grylloblattids live on glaciers and snowfields, scavenging on windblown scraps of food. Their body processes are adapted to thrive at temperatures of about 0 to 5° Celsius. If they become much warmer they die.

A grylloblattid.

Extremes of heat and cold

The water of some hot springs is too scalding to touch. Yet **extremophile** organisms like **bacteria** and **algae** grow and form crusts on the rocks. At the other end of the temperature scale are cold-loving ice-worms (*Mesenchytraeus*) which burrow through the ice of Alaska, and bacteria that live on the undersides of icebergs. These simple organisms contain unusual versions of the normal substances called **enzymes**, which break down minerals in the surroundings to get the energy for life.

Hot springs support colourful heat-loving organisms.

The urban jungle

The fastest-spreading **habitat** in the world is the **urban** one of towns and cities. Bricks, concrete, tarmac and mown grass may seem hostile and forbidding to wild animals and plants. Indeed most cannot survive here. But the urban habitat has some features that are similar to certain natural surroundings. This is why certain plants and animals have **adapted** to town and city life. Others have done so well that we regard them as pests.

City cliffs and crags

In the wild, rock doves live and nest around cliffs and crags. The urban habitat has 'cliffs' too — the walls and ledges of buildings. This similarity led rock doves to move into towns, where they feasted on leftovers and waste food. Gradually they became urban inhabitants. Today hundreds of major cities have large populations of their descendants, known as **feral** or town pigeons.

At home in the town

This story has been repeated for various kinds of animals and plants that are now familiar town and city dwellers. Creatures include house mice, brown rats, grey squirrels, red foxes, gulls, starlings, house sparrows, blackbirds, spiders, ants, termites, cockroaches and the commonest of all, house flies and similar flies. In many tropical regions animals such as geckos and tree frogs also frequent houses. Plants include nettles, plantains ,willowherbs, and shrubs like elder and buddleia.

Birds like this robin will happily nest in quiet buildings or sheds.

Taking the opportunity

The wildlife that moves into towns and cities is **opportunistic**. It takes the opportunity or chance to live in the surroundings we create for ourselves. All the essentials of life are here, such as warmth in our centrally-heated buildings, and shelter in our roof spaces, hollow walls, pipes and drains. And of course plentiful food, either stored for our use or thrown away in trash bins and on rubbish heaps. The animals are adaptable too. They change their behaviour and diet, taking the opportunity to eat what is available and nest wherever they can.

Up in the roof

Barns, churches and other big buildings are like great tree holes or caves for animals. They have been taken over by different animals in different parts of the world:

- Racoons in North America.
- Roof rats in parts of Asia.
- Ring-tailed possums in Australia.
- Barn owls in most places, making the barn owl the world's most widespread bird.

Did you know?

One of the world's biggest feathered pests is the red-billed quelea. Millions of these birds devastate farm crops all across the continent of Africa.

Many animals, especially those that **scavenge** in their natural habitats like gulls and rats, fit in well in urban habitats. The refuse tip is like a vast supermarket for them, full of all kinds of wonderful foods.

Glossary

adapted, adaptation a feature of a living thing that helps it to fit into its surroundings, or environment, and improve its chances of survival

algae simple plants without proper flowers, stems or roots. They include seaweeds of all kinds and also the tiny plants, phytoplankton.

anti-freeze a chemical substance that does not freeze solid when it becomes very cold

bacteria minute living things, only visible under a microscope, and found almost everywhere on Earth

blubber an oily or fatty layer under the skin of certain animals, which helps to keep in body warmth

camouflage blending in with the surroundings, usually by shape, colour and pattern, to be less noticeable

cold-blooded a creature whose body temperature varies with the temperature of its surroundings

colony a group of living things that are fairly close together in one area

corms an underground part of a plant similar to a bulb. During winter the plant dies down and the corm stores all the plant's nutrients until spring when the plant will grow again.

dormant 'sleeping' – still, inactive and not changing much

drought a long time without rain or some other form of moisture, as in a desert environment

enzymes natural chemical substances inside living things that cause changes inside the body, such as breaking down or digesting food to obtain energy

ephemeral short-lived, fleeting, soon gone

epiphytic a plant which grows on another one and uses it to gain height, support and perhaps shelter

estuary a river's mouth, where it opens out wide and flows into the sea

extremophile a living thing which thrives in extreme or exceptional conditions such as great heat or intense cold

feral animals which were once tame or domesticated but which have escaped to become wild again

gills feathery parts of an animal such as a fish, designed to obtain oxygen dissolved in water

habitat a distinctive type of place or surroundings, such as a woodland, mountain top, grassland, pond or seashore

haemoglobin a red substance in the blood or similar body fluid of an animal, specialized to absorb and carry oxygen around the body

hibernate when an animal becomes very inactive and goes into a 'deep sleep' during a cold time, and its body processes slow down

krill small sea creatures similar to shrimps or prawns and in the same main animal group (crustaceans)

larva   the young form or stage of an animal, which is usually different in shape from the adult, and which spends much time feeding

meanders   wide curves or bends in a river where it gently 'wanders' across a flat region

migrate, migration   a long journey usually undertaken by animals with the changing seasons, to find improved conditions such as more food or better shelter

nocturnal   active at night, during the hours of darkness

nutrients   substances needed by a living thing for its growth, development and survival

opportunistic   taking any chance or opportunity that comes along

organism   a living thing

parasite   a living thing that obtains some requirement such as food or shelter from another, called the host, and harms the host in the process

phytoplankton   tiny plants drifting in the water (see zooplankton)

pioneer   being one of the first or earliest in a new or strange place

prairies   large regions of grassland where there are few trees, especially in North America

predators   living things which hunt, catch and kill other living things, their prey, for food

rakers   comb-like parts on the gills of a water animal, which filter or sieve tiny bits of food from the water

scavenge   to search for and eat dead or dying living things, remains of other predators' kills, or leftover food

siphon   in an animal, a body opening shaped like a tube that takes water in or passes it out, usually for breathing or feeding

species   a group of living things that look similar to each other and can breed together, but which cannot breed with other living things

spermaceti   a waxy or oily substance inside the head of the sperm whale that helps it to dive to great depths

stagnant   still, old or stale, rather than fresh and new – like the water in an old ditch

symbiosis   when two different kinds (species) of living things survive together and help or benefit each other

swim bladder   the body part of a water creature such as a fish which contains bubbles of gas and helps the animal to swim, rise and descend

temperate   average conditions, neither too hot nor too cold – usually referring to areas of the Earth which are neither really hot like the tropics or really cold like the poles

tundra   flat, treeless region in a very cold place, where the soil is frozen for part of the year

urban   to do with towns, cities or built up areas

warm-blooded   a creature whose body temperature is controlled from within and stays fairly constant, usually above the temperature of the creature's surroundings

zooplankton   tiny animals drifting in the water (see phytoplankton)

Index